This Coloring book Belongs To:

....

....

....

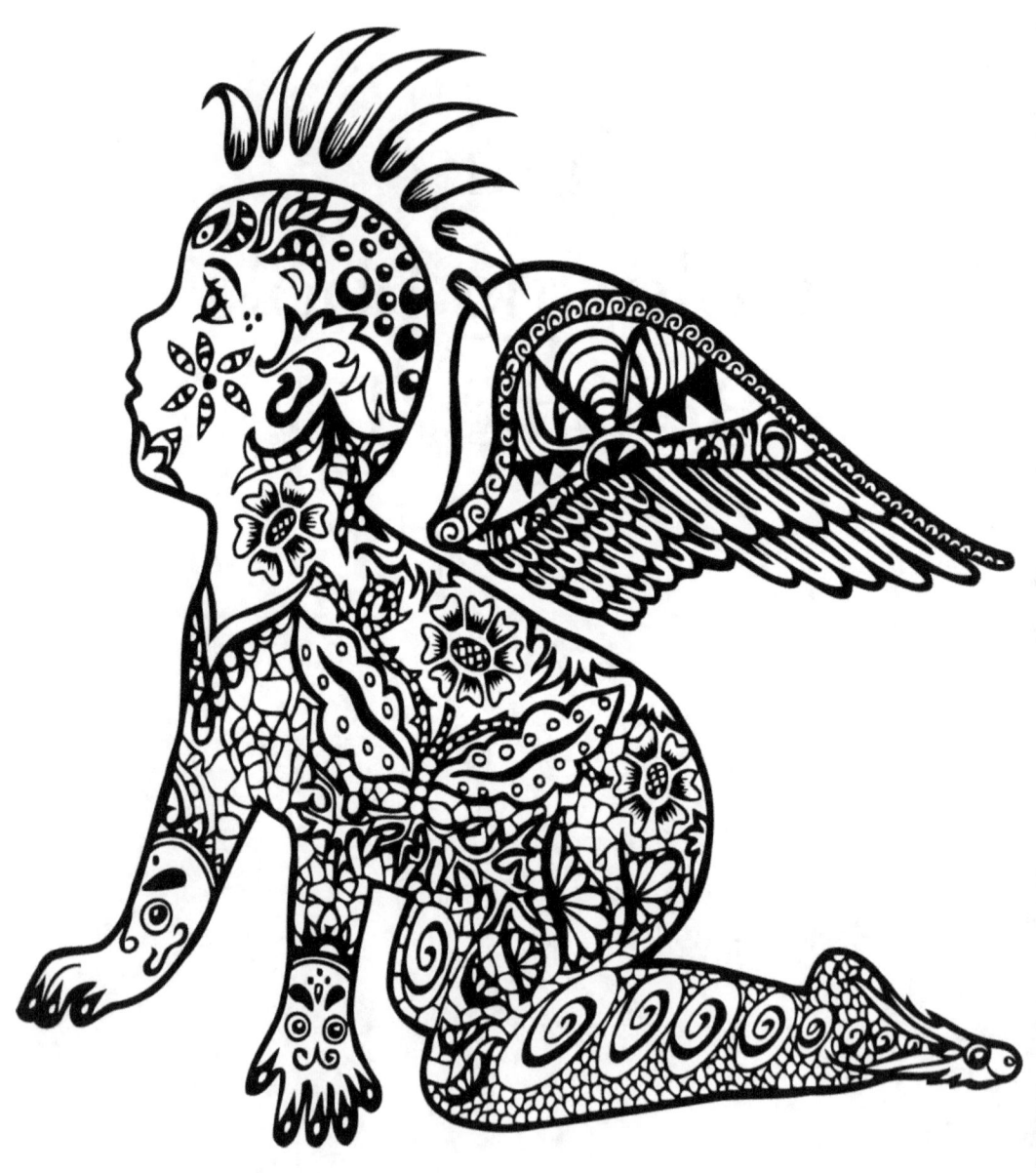

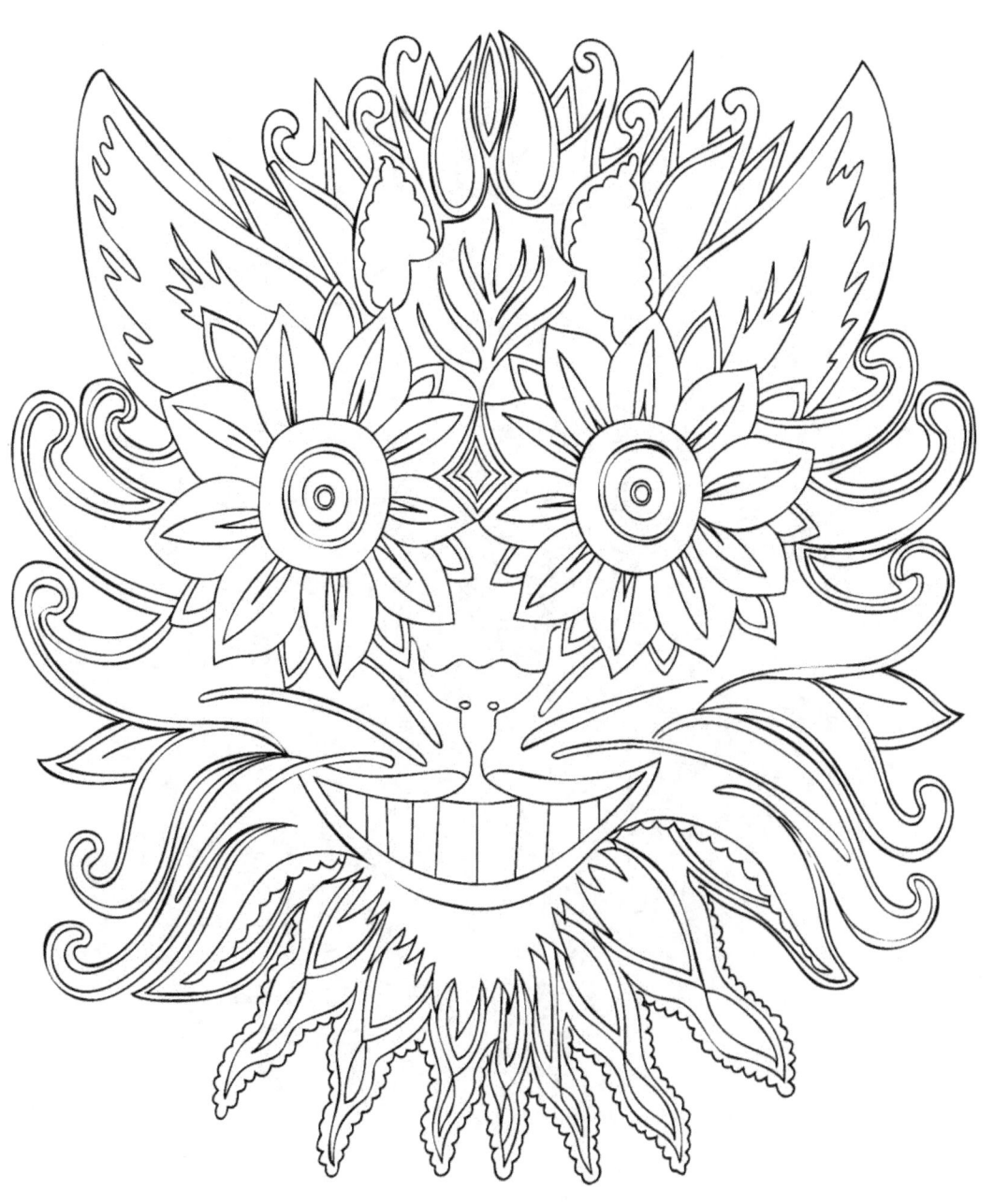

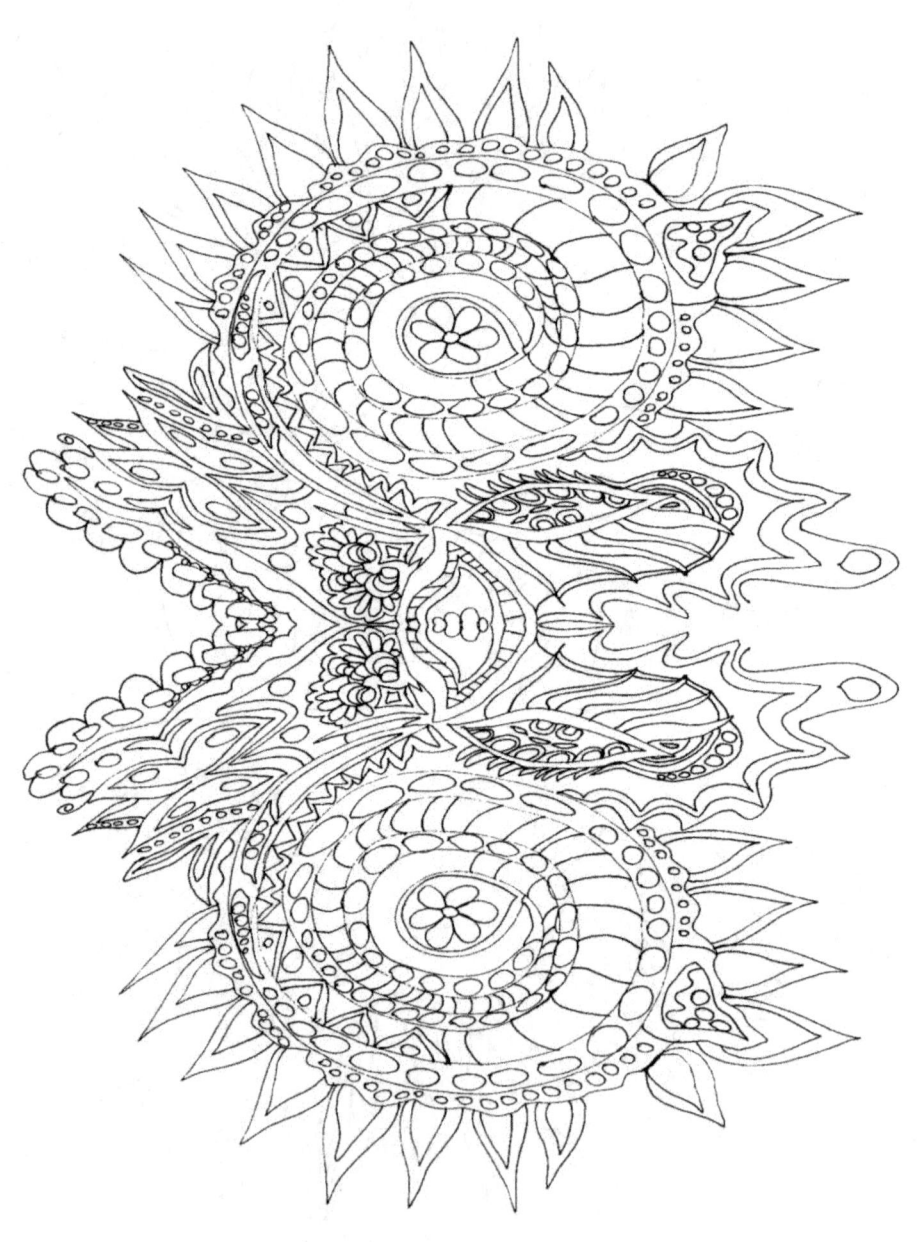

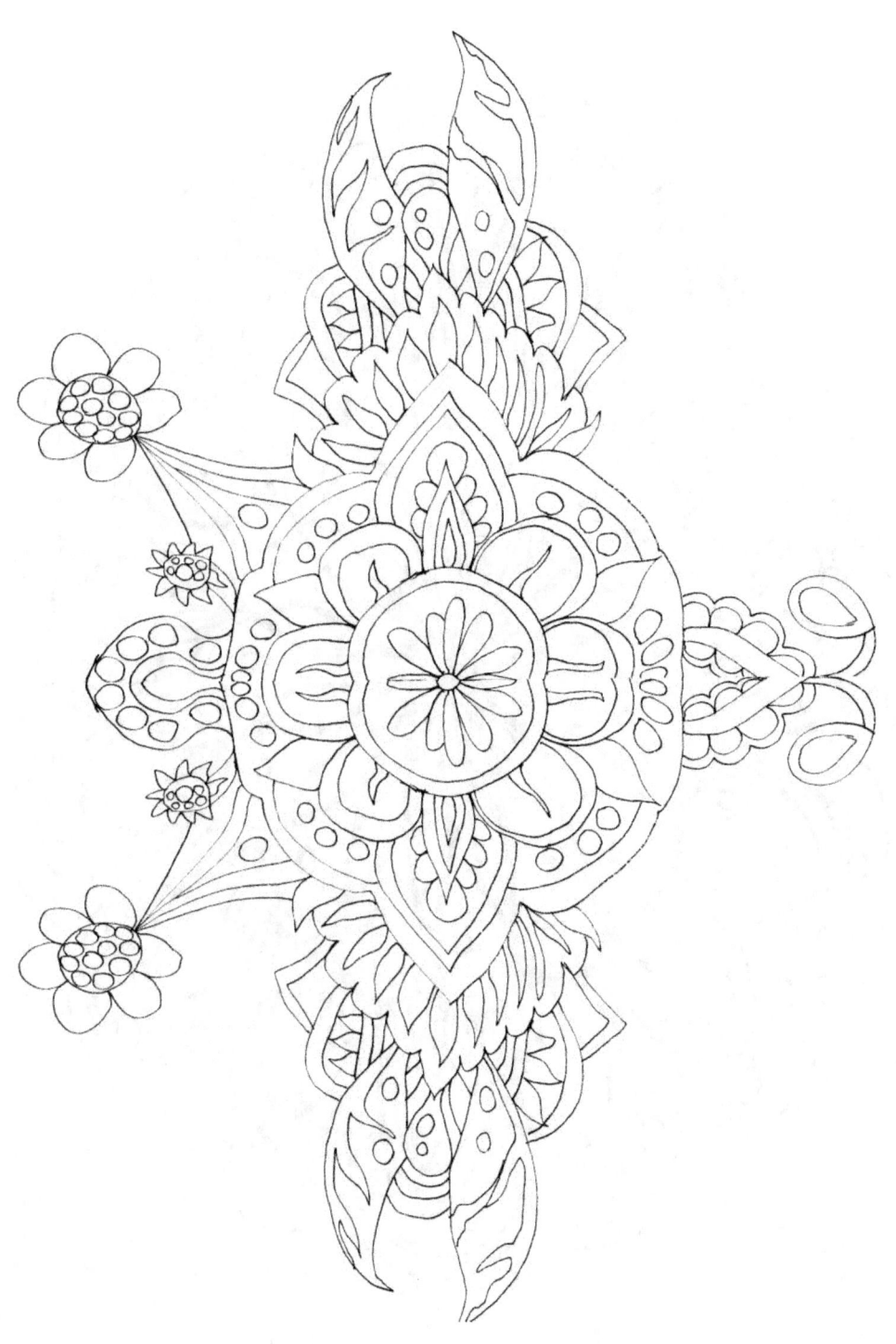

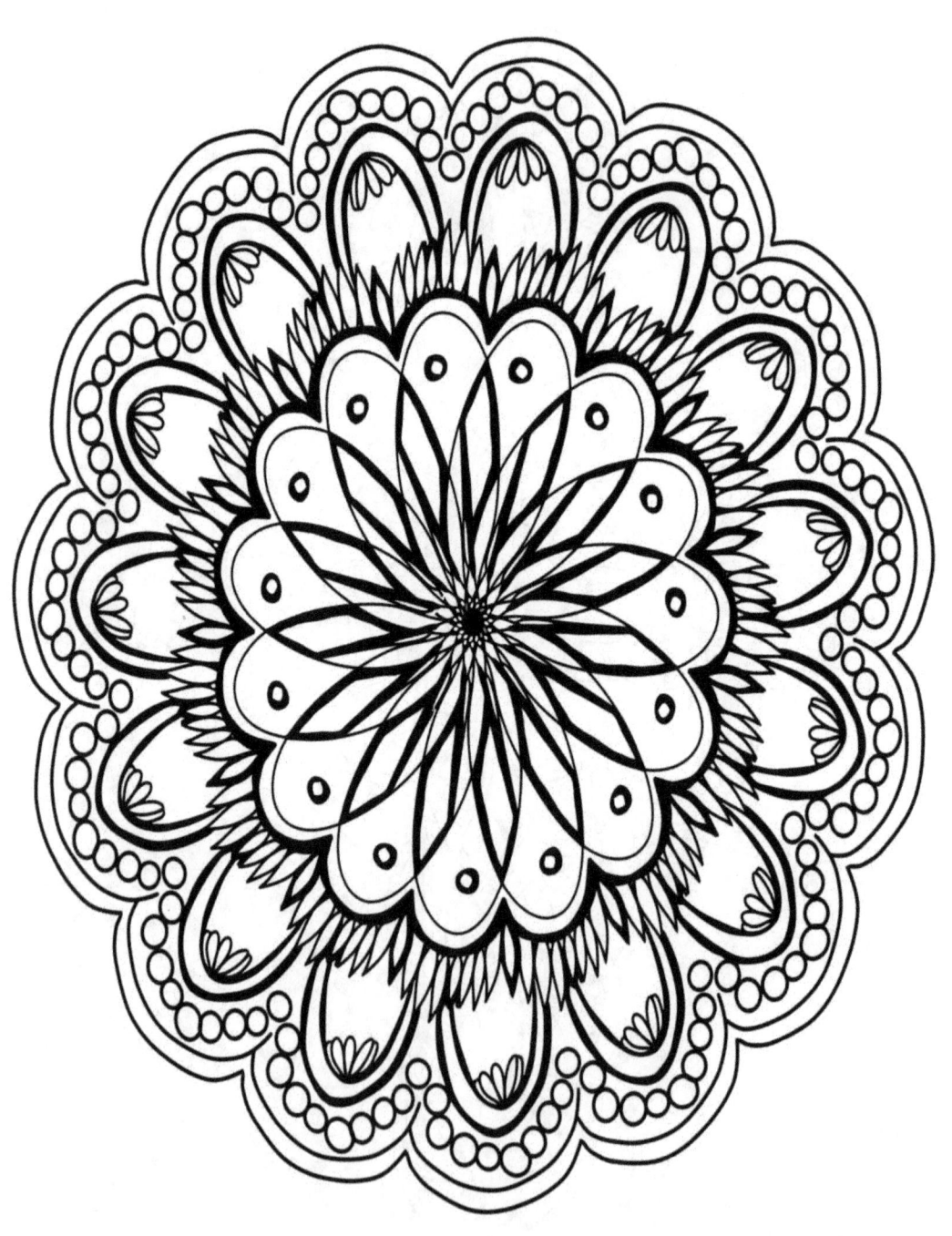

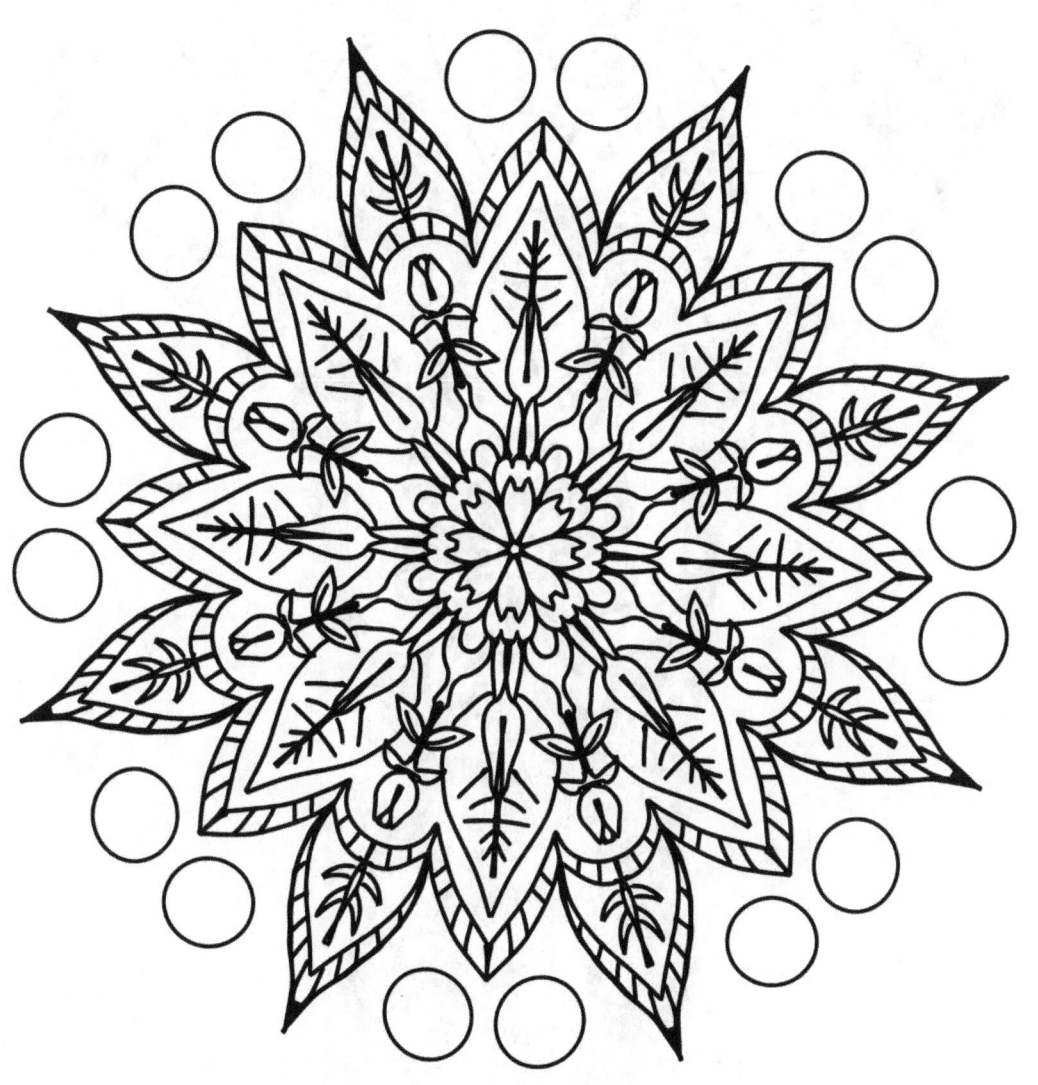

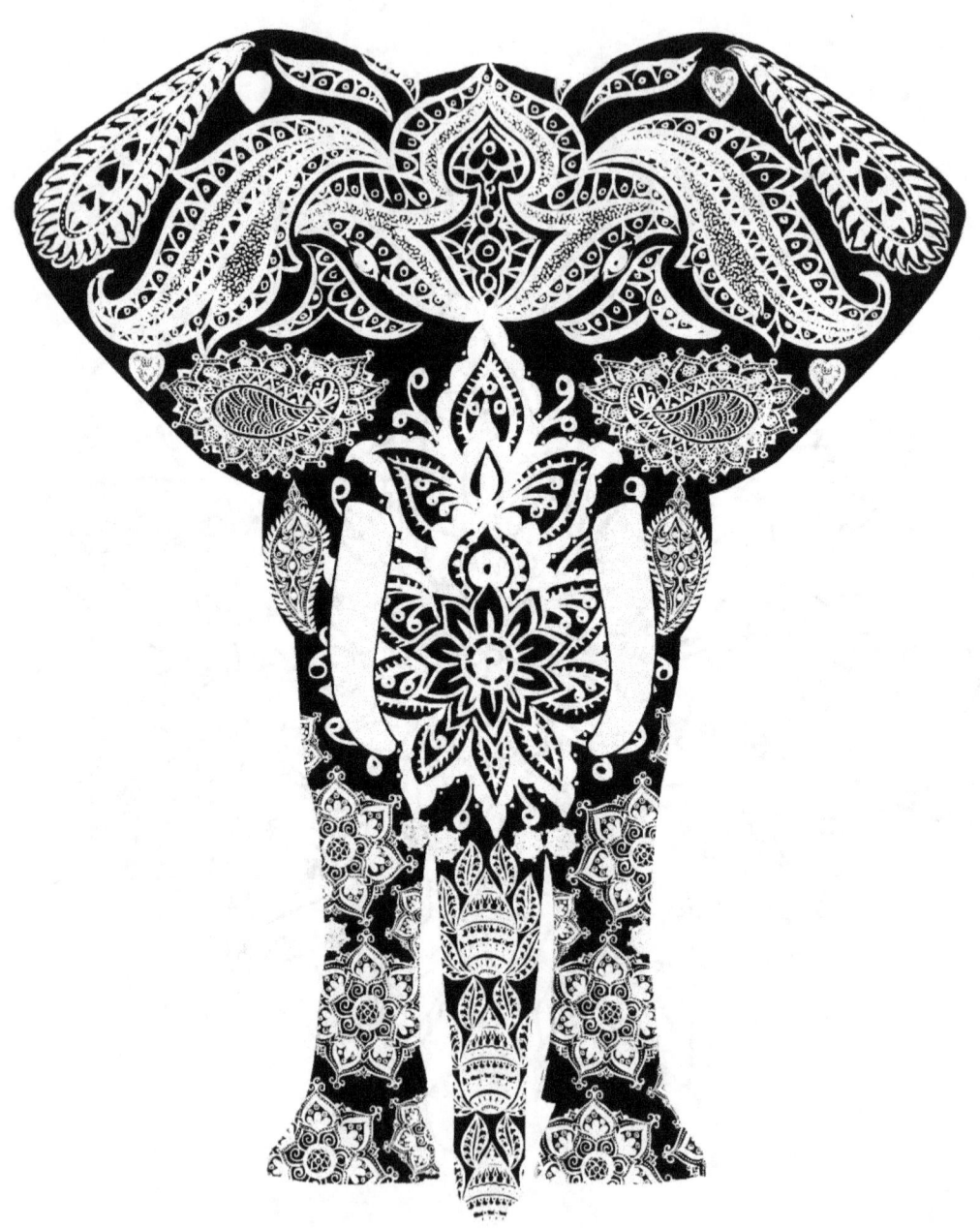

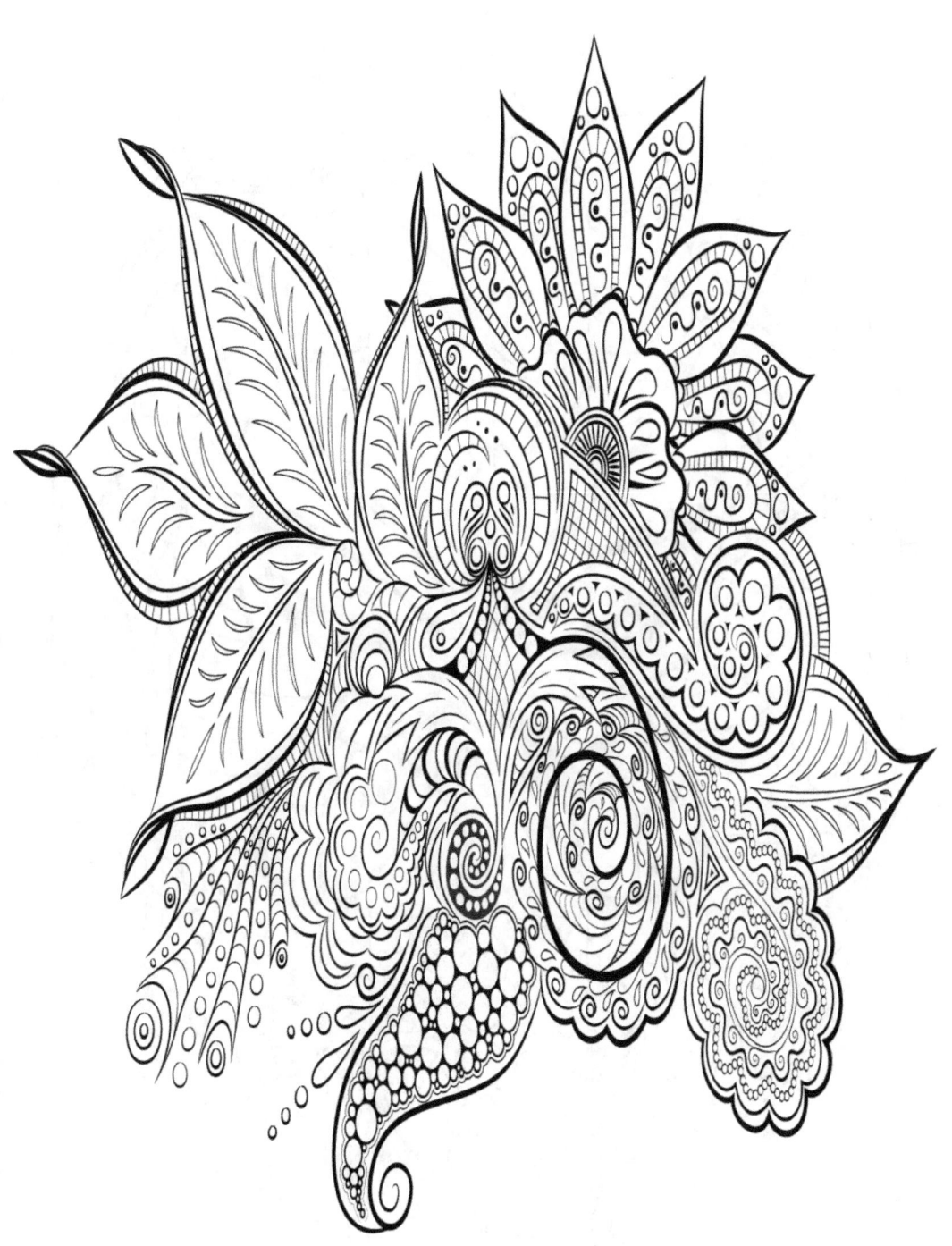

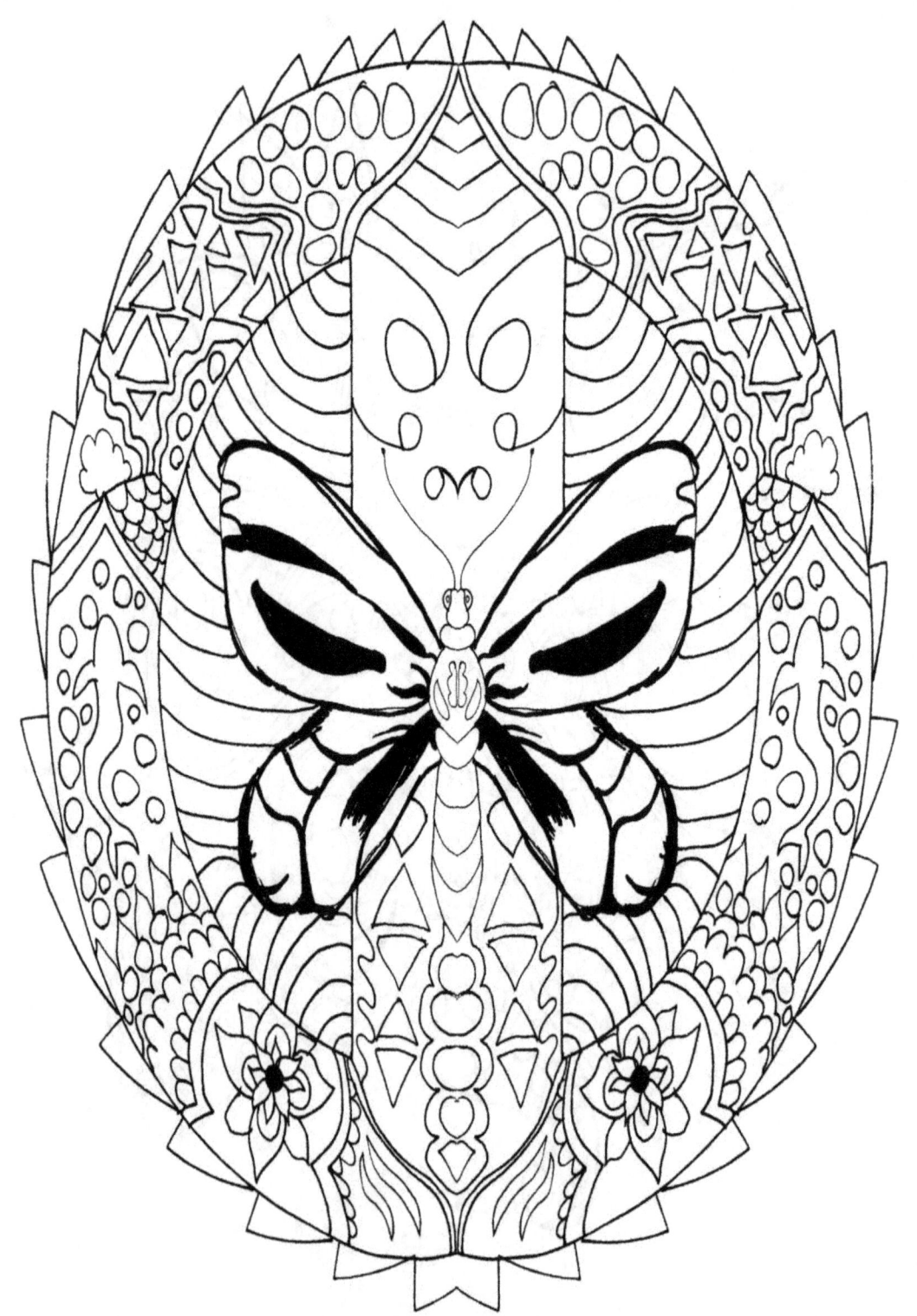

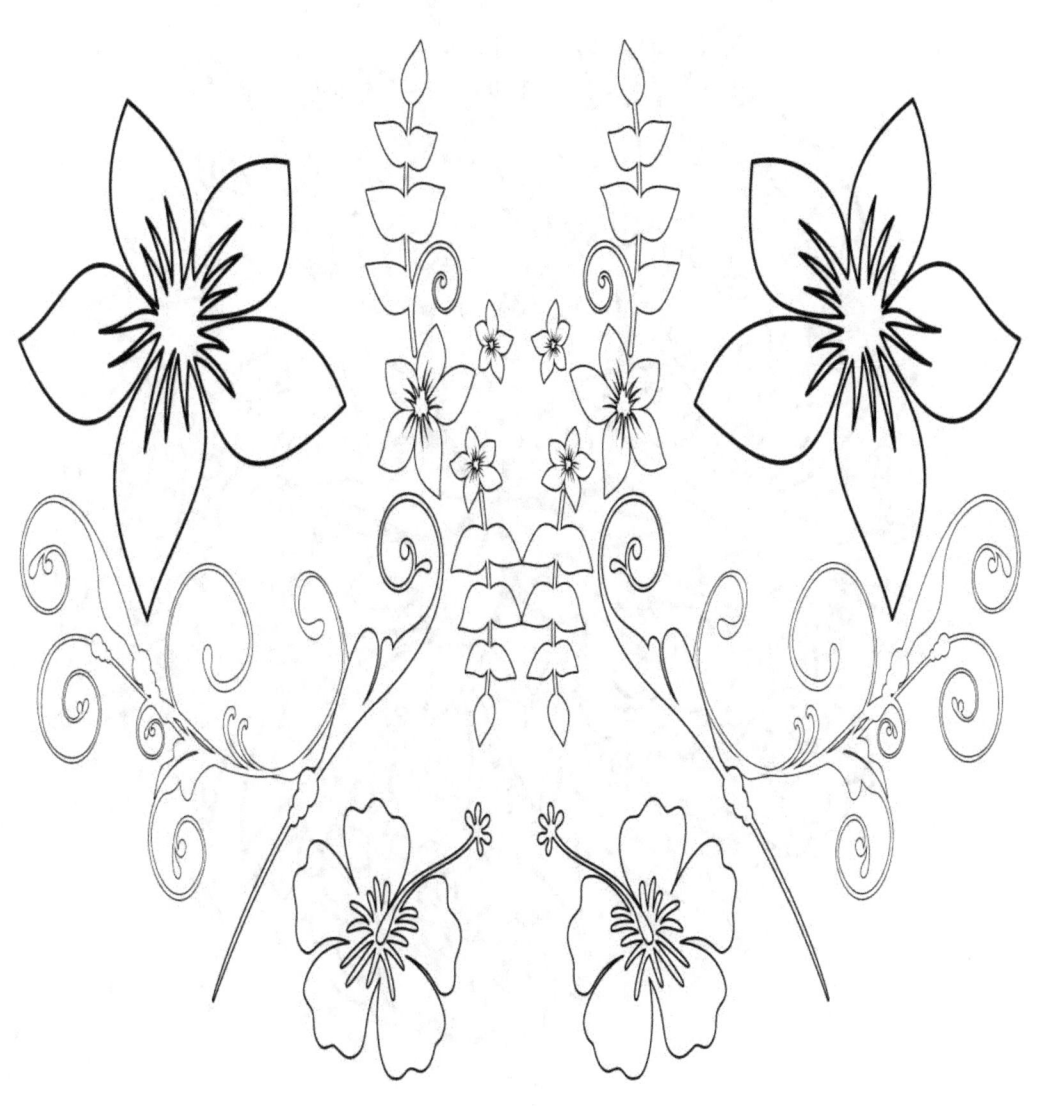

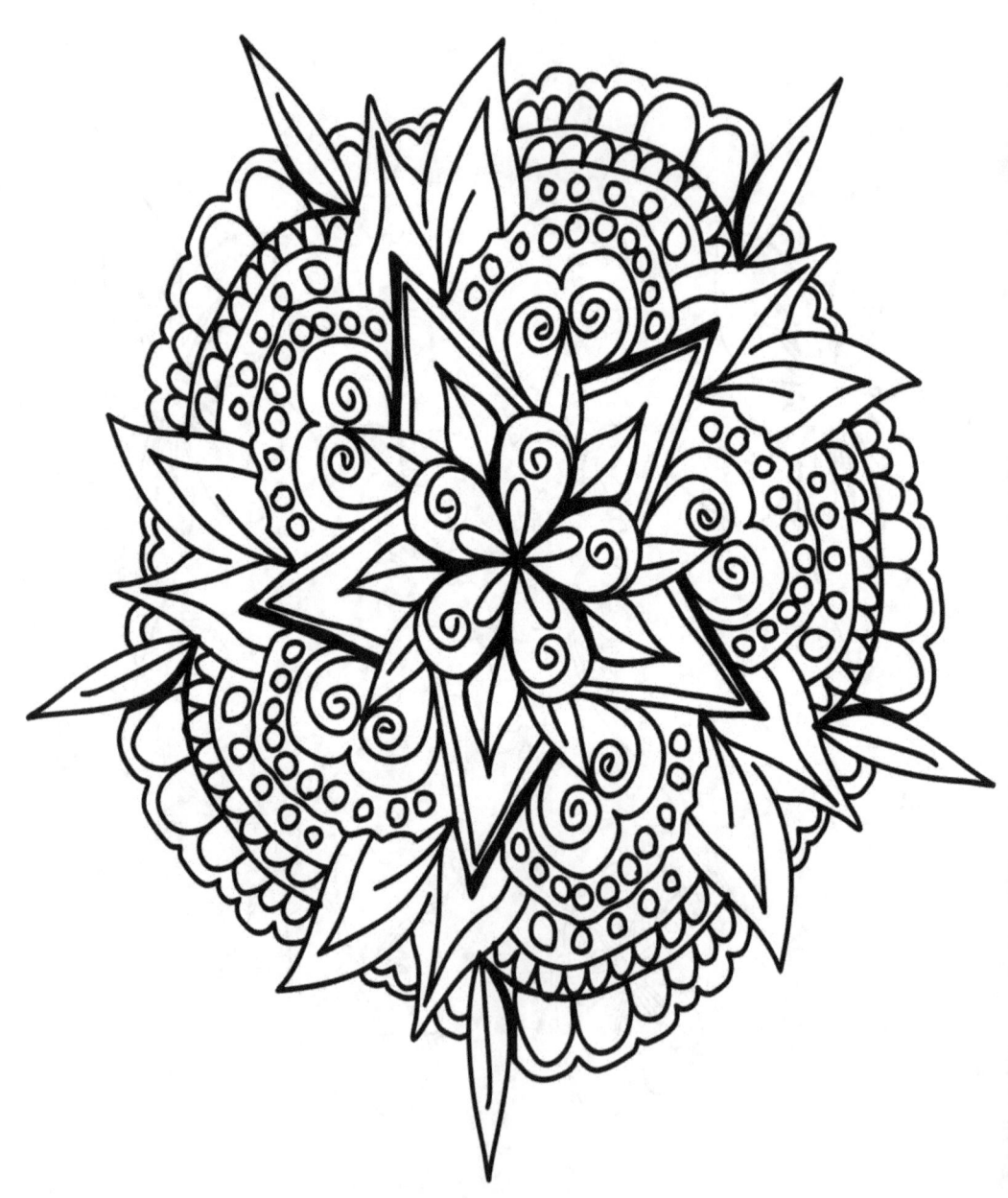

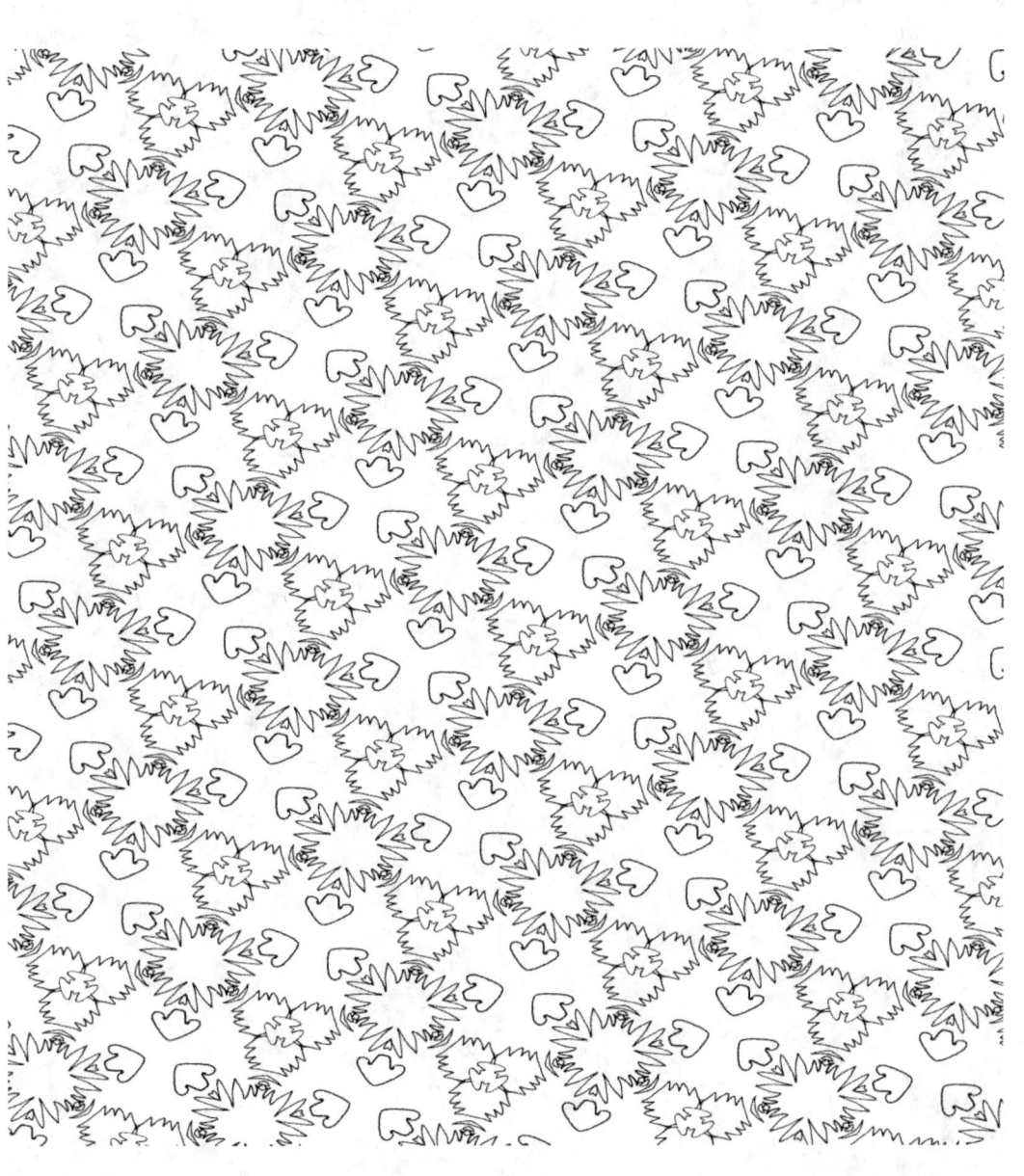

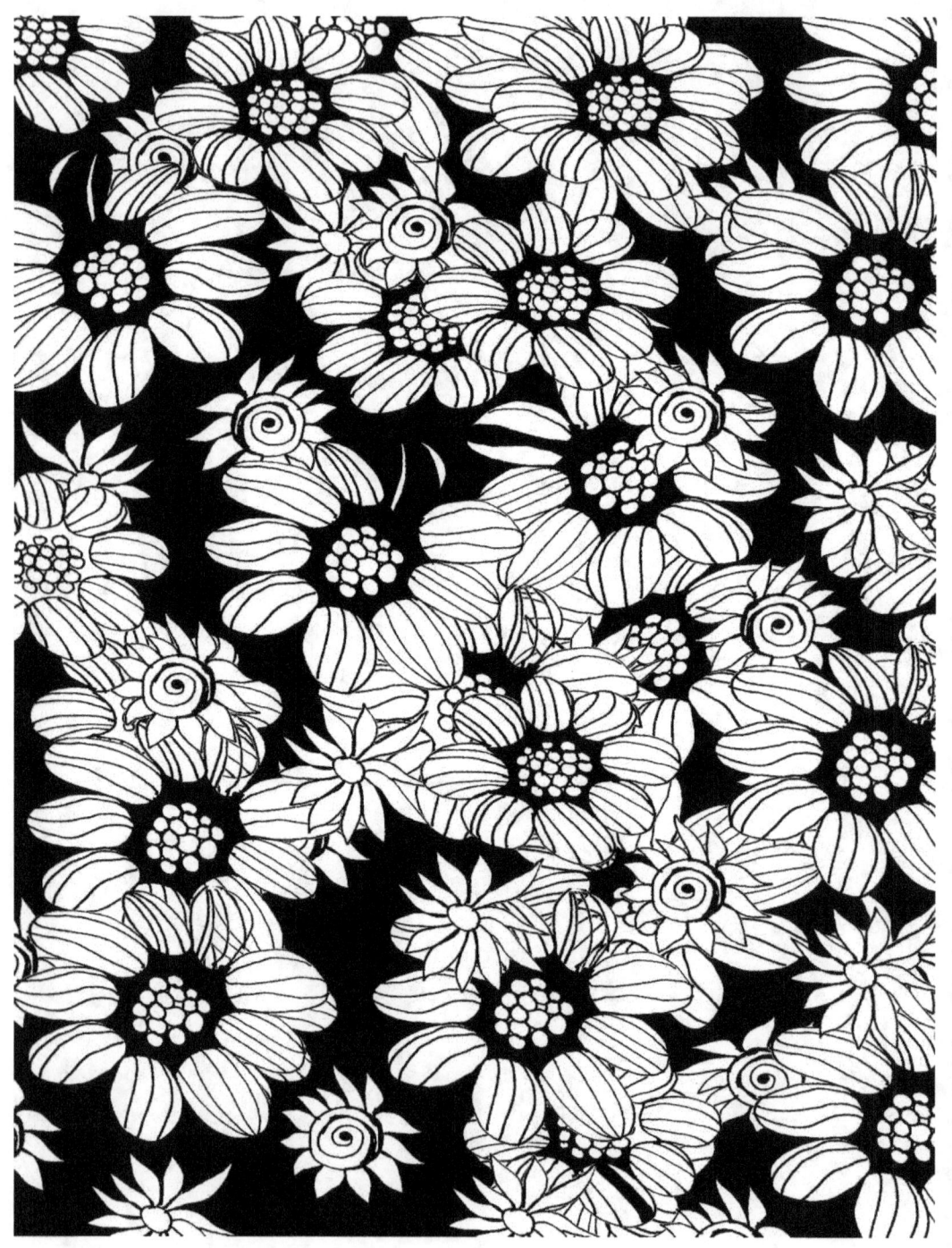

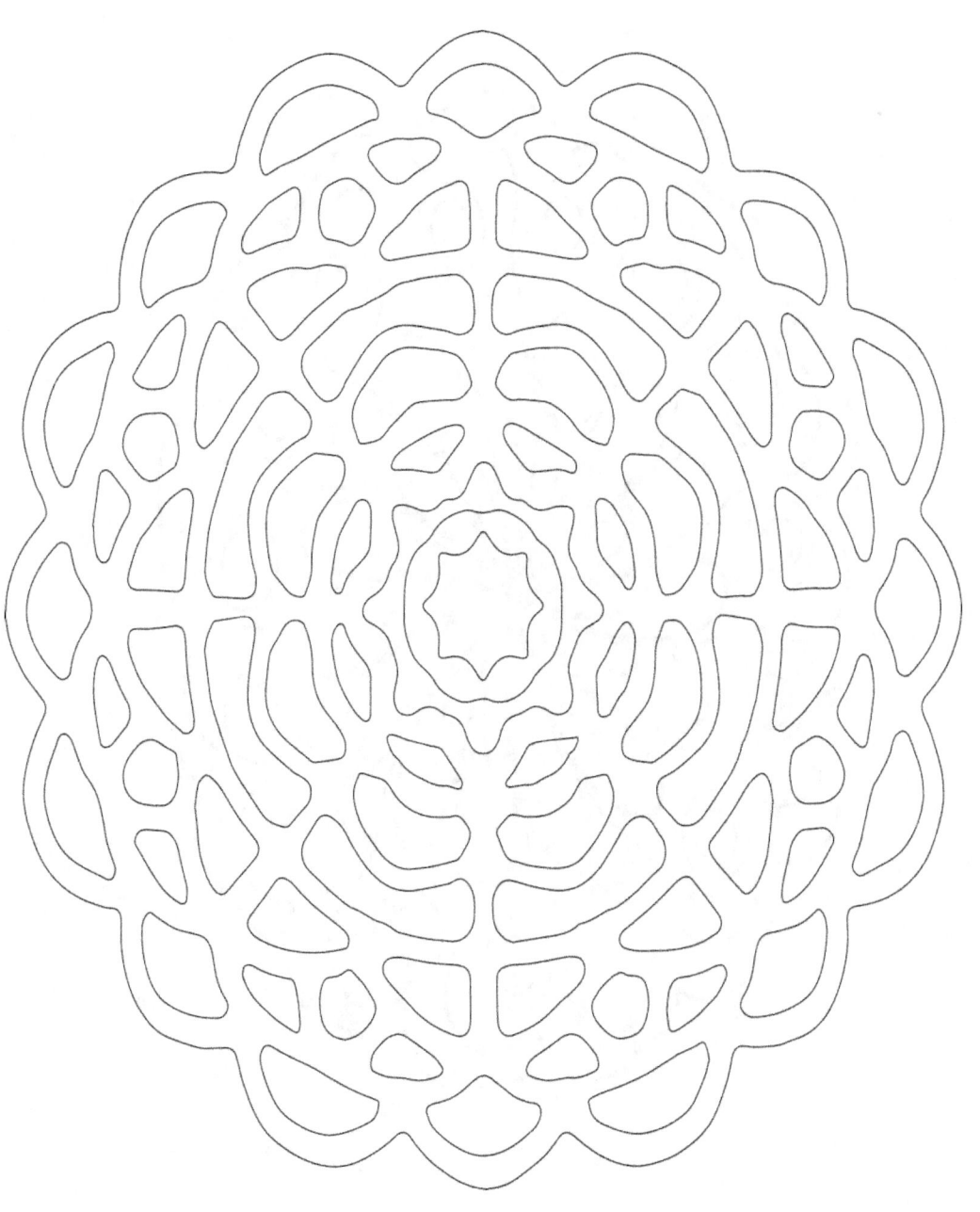

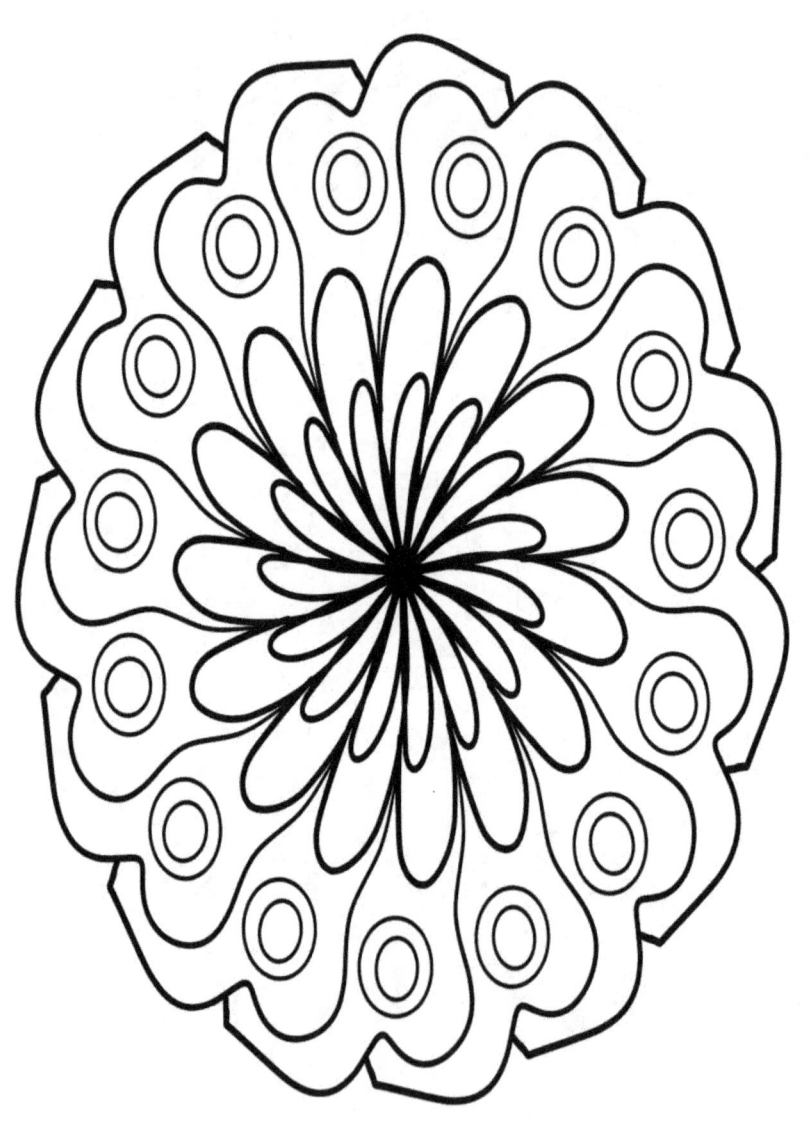

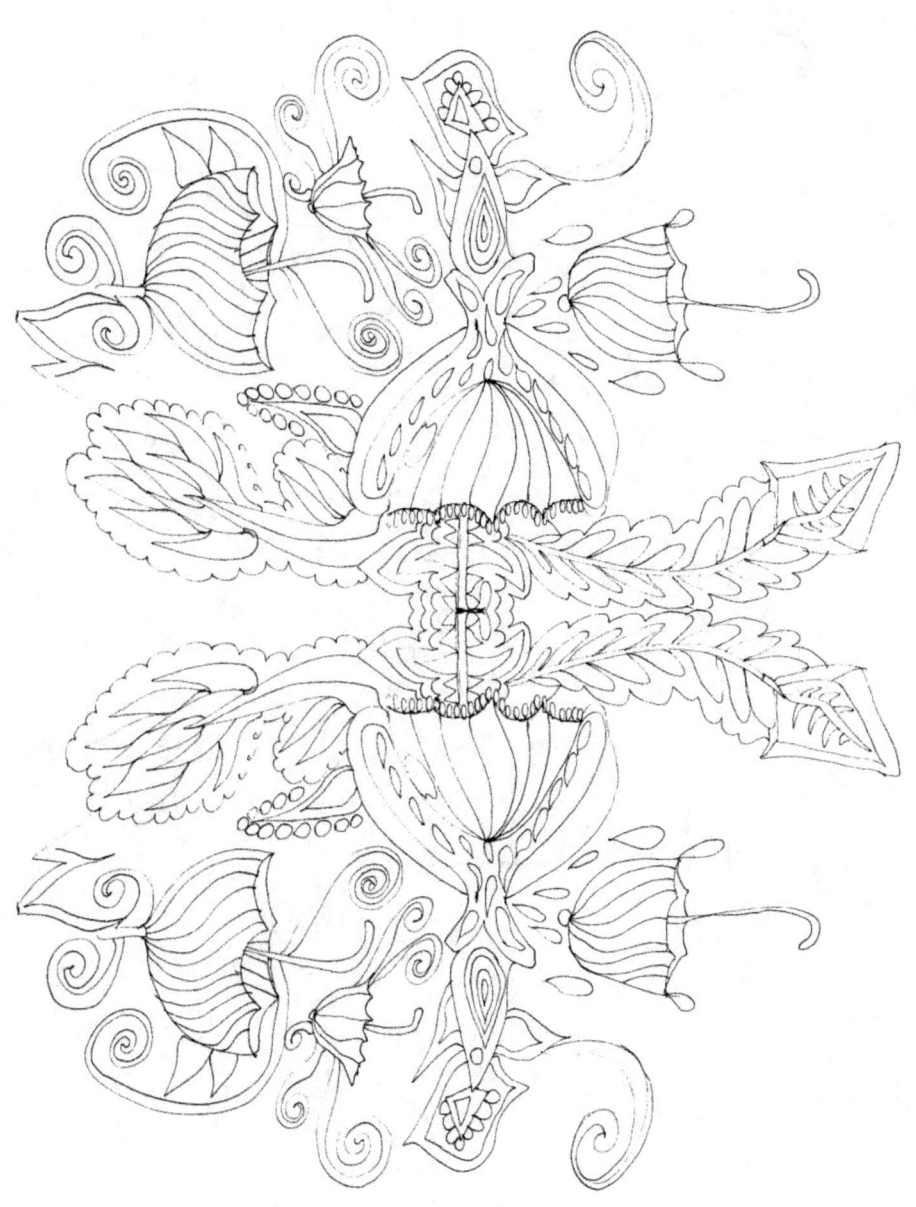

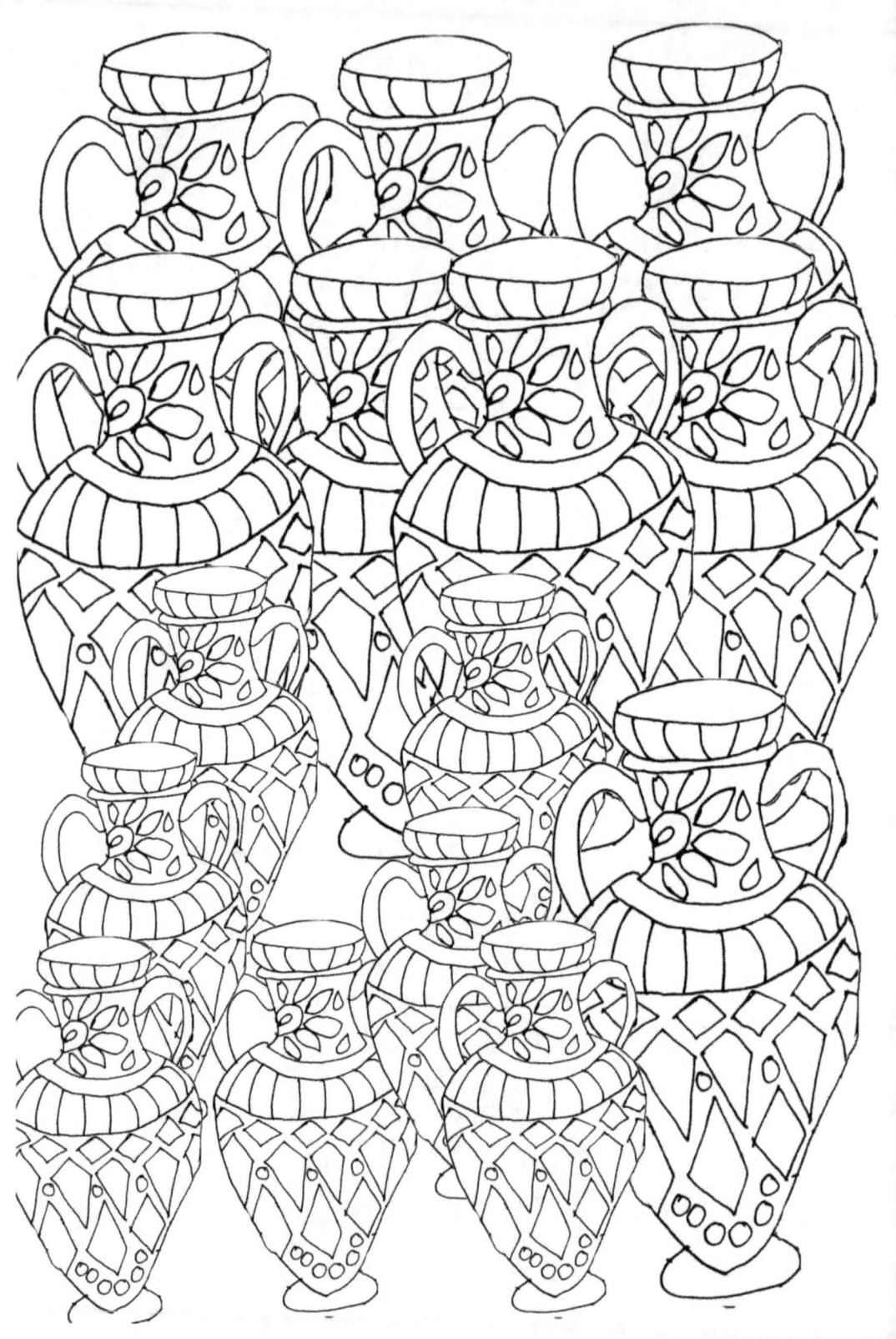

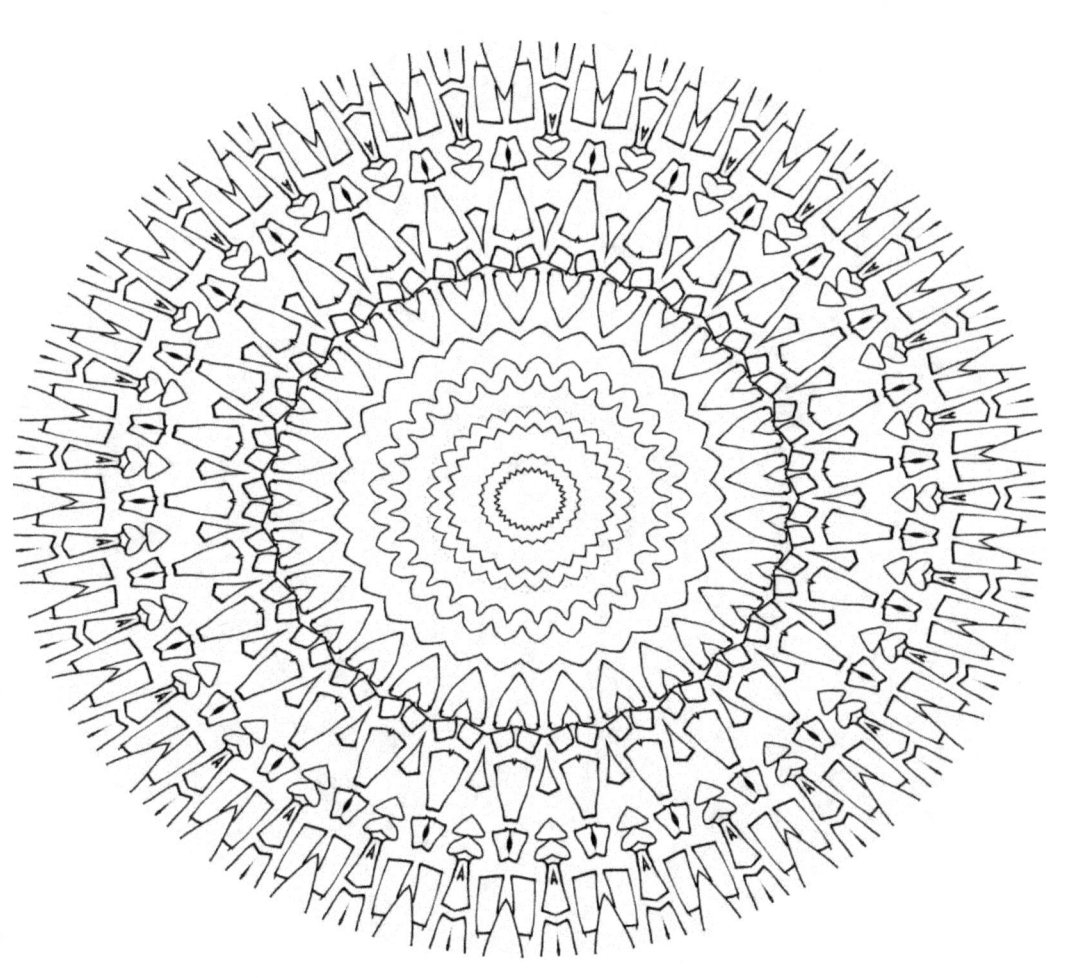

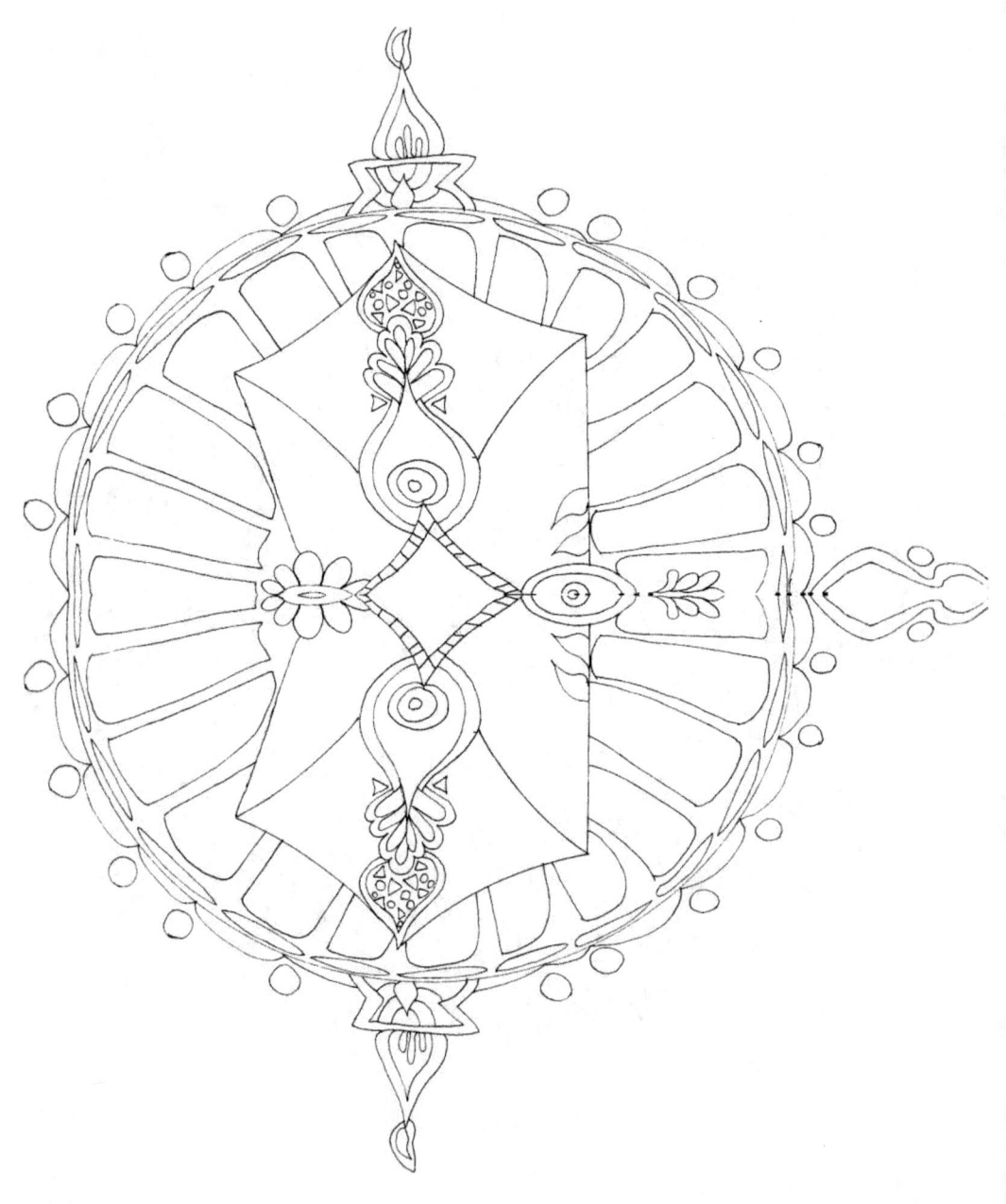

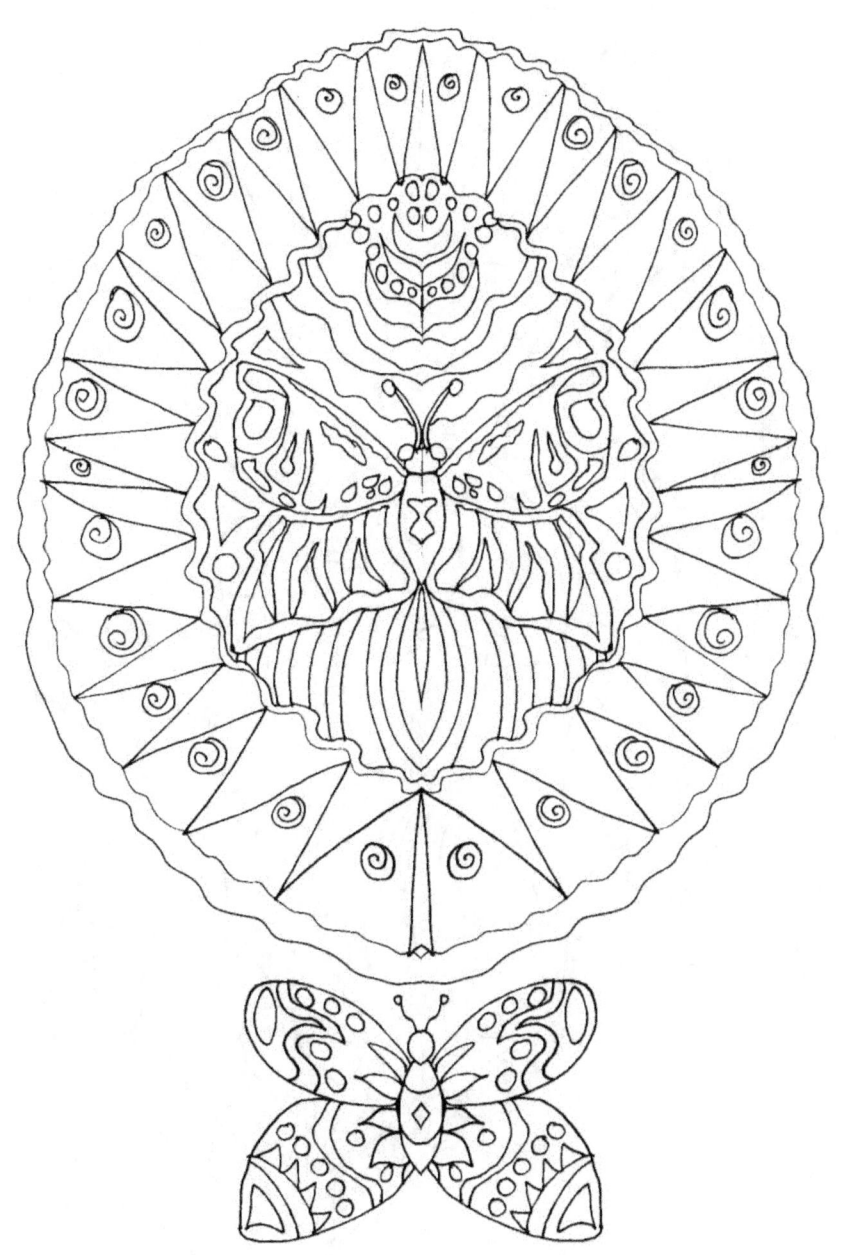

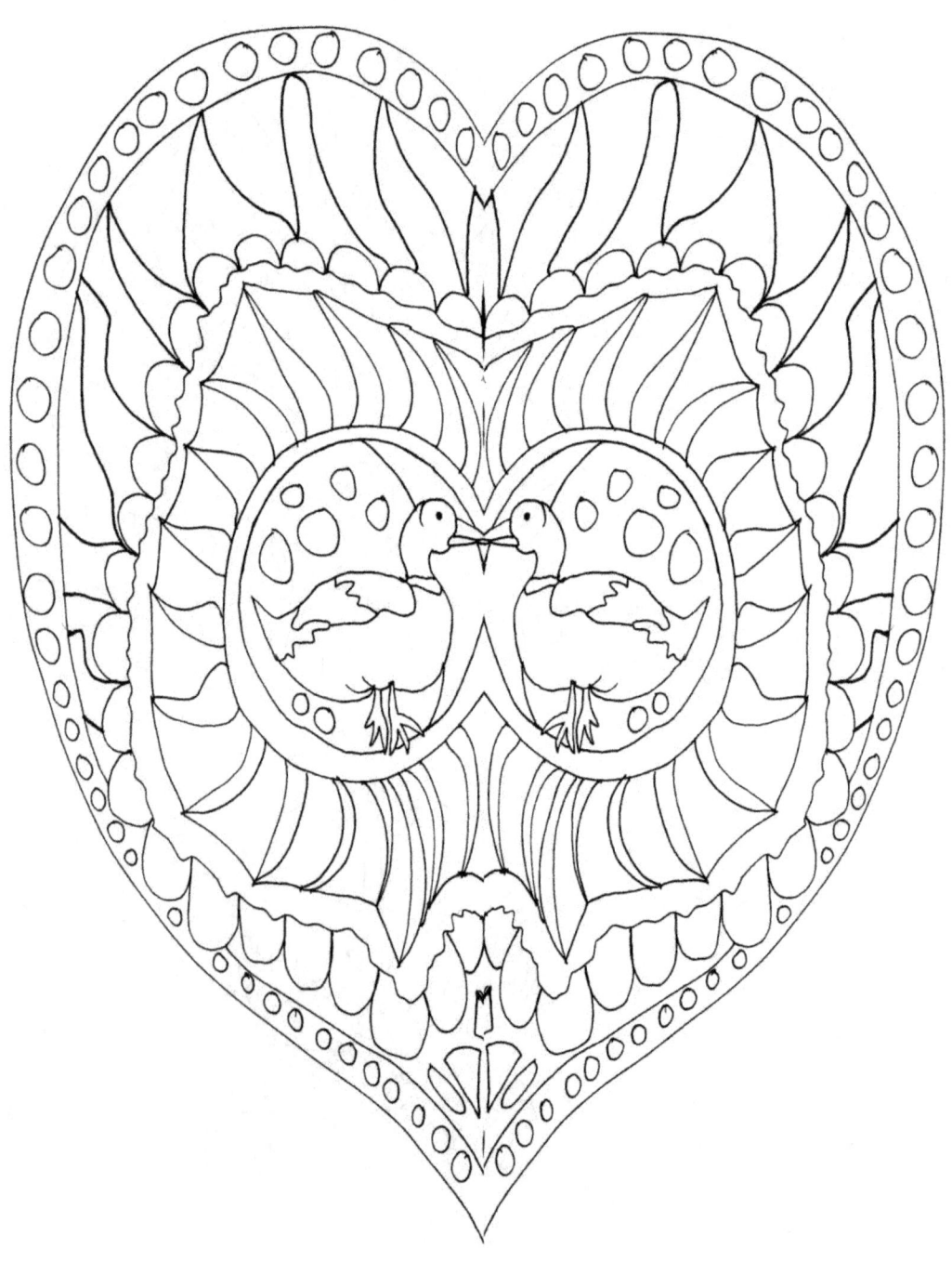

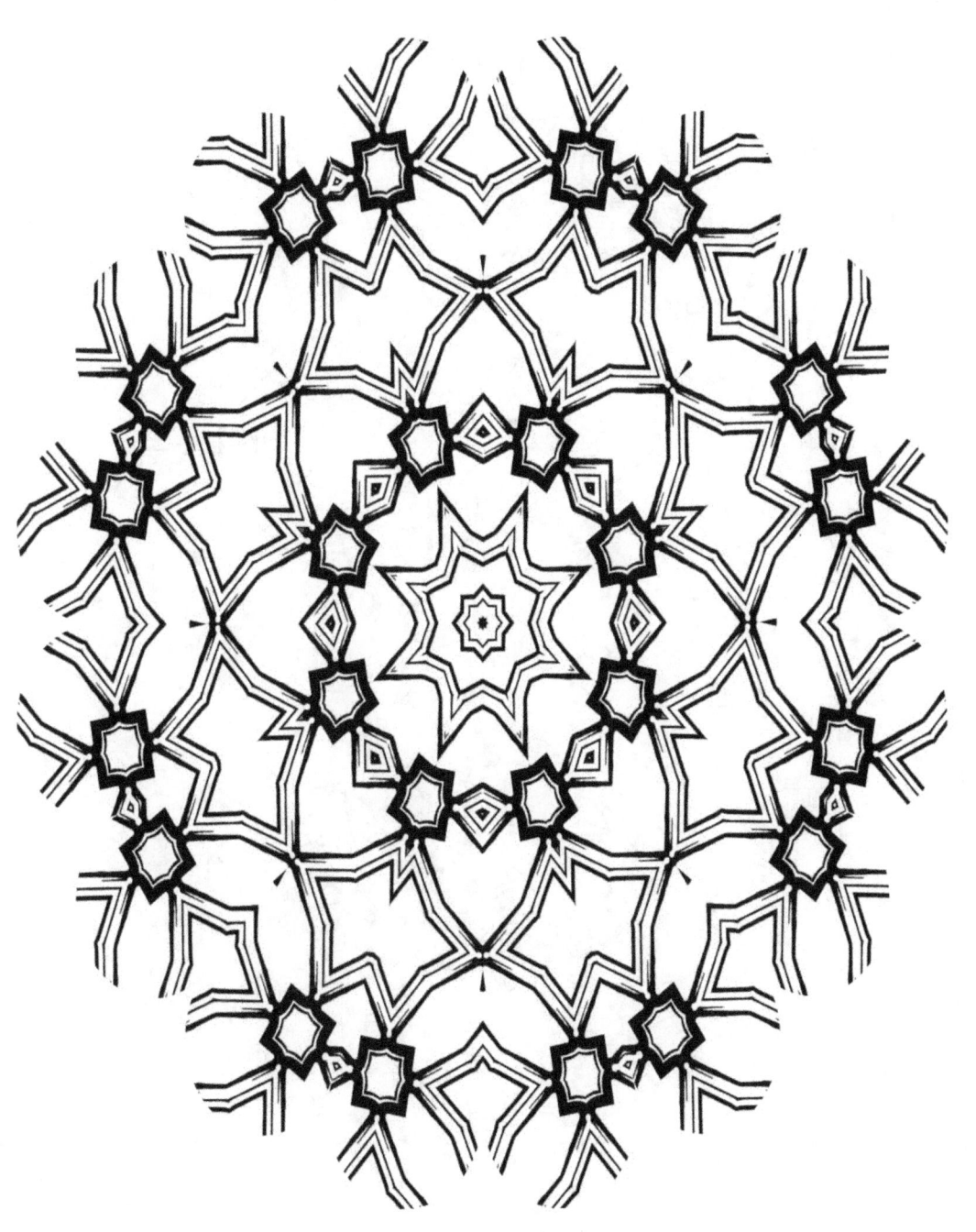

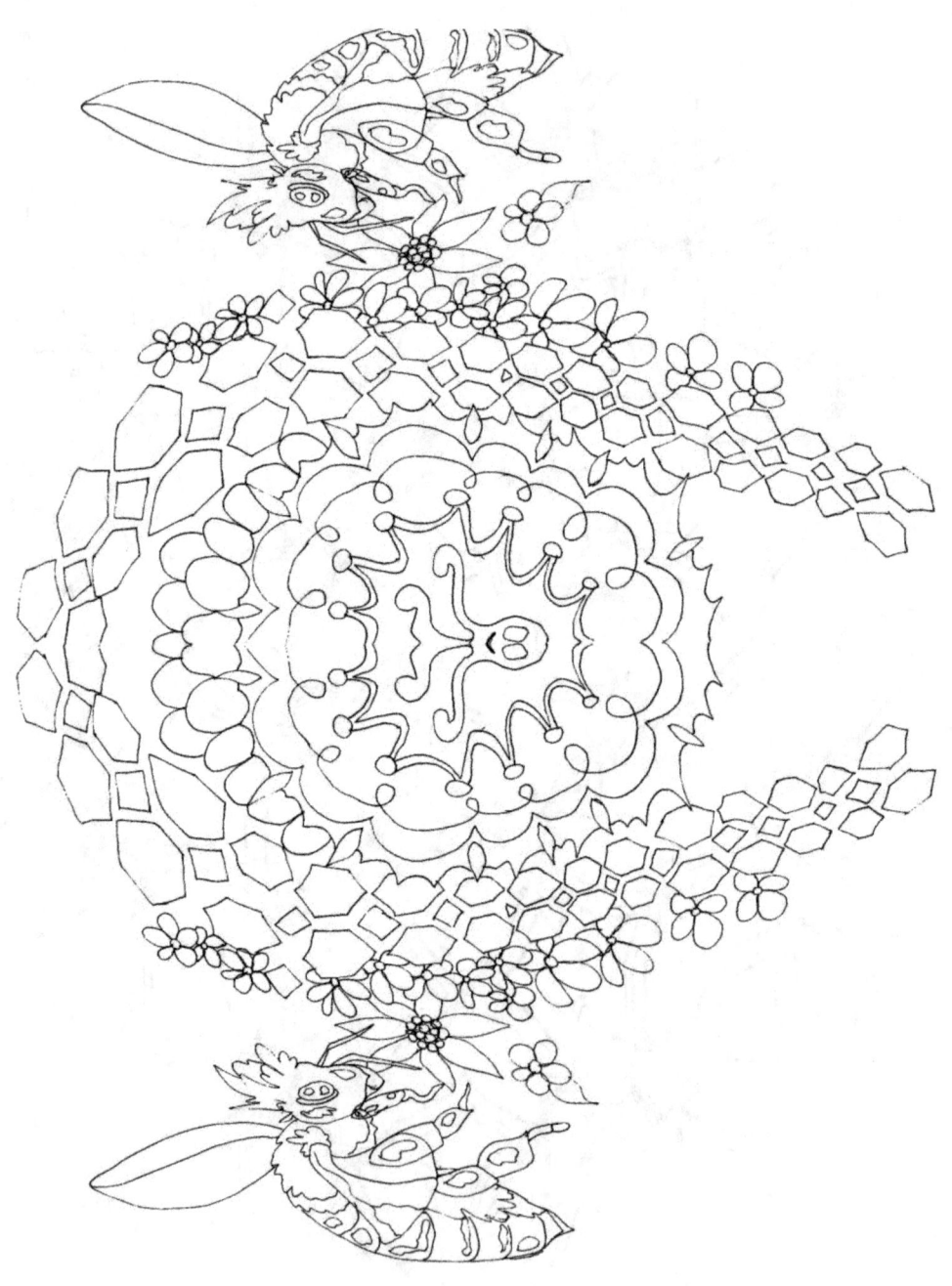

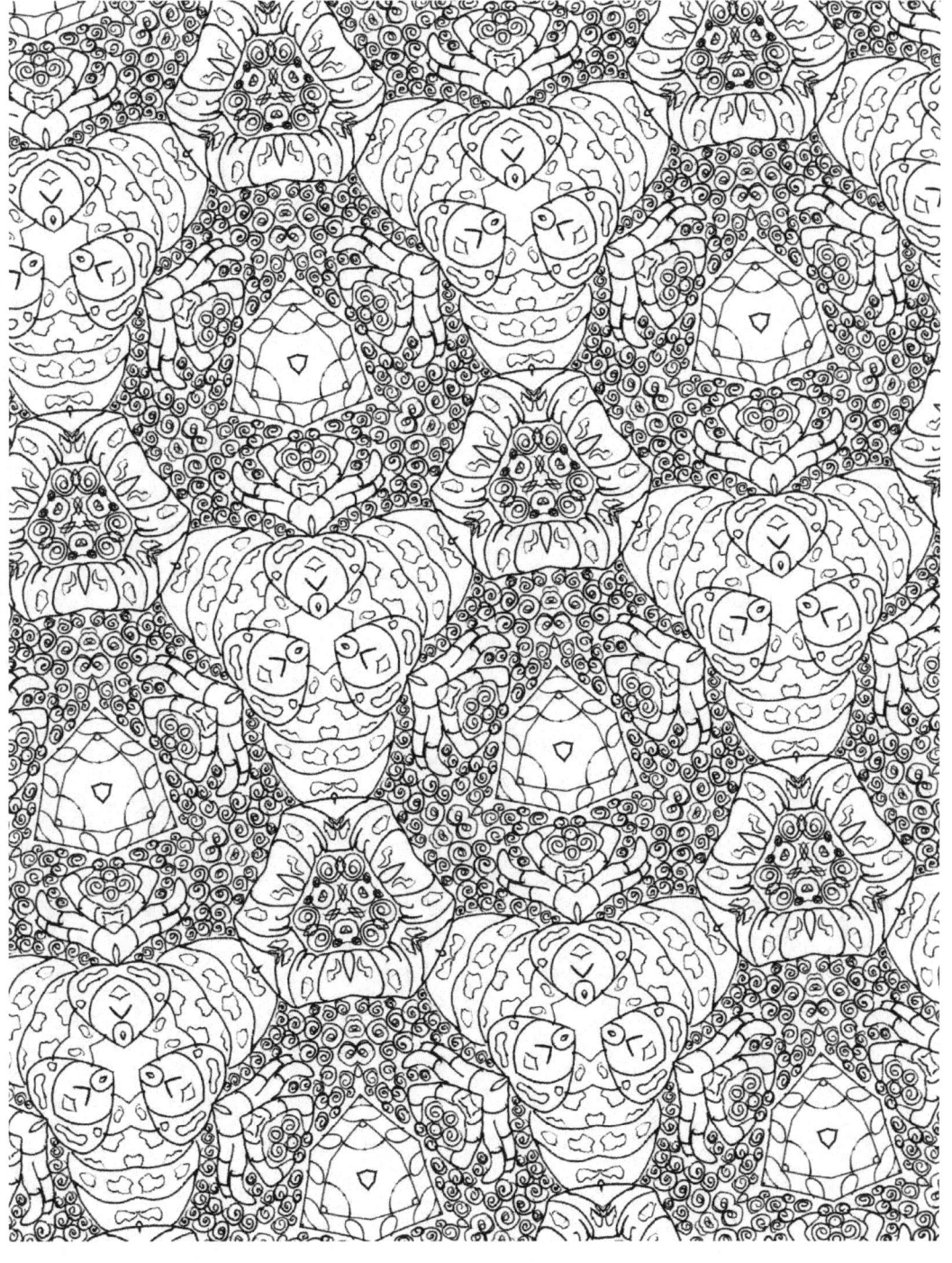

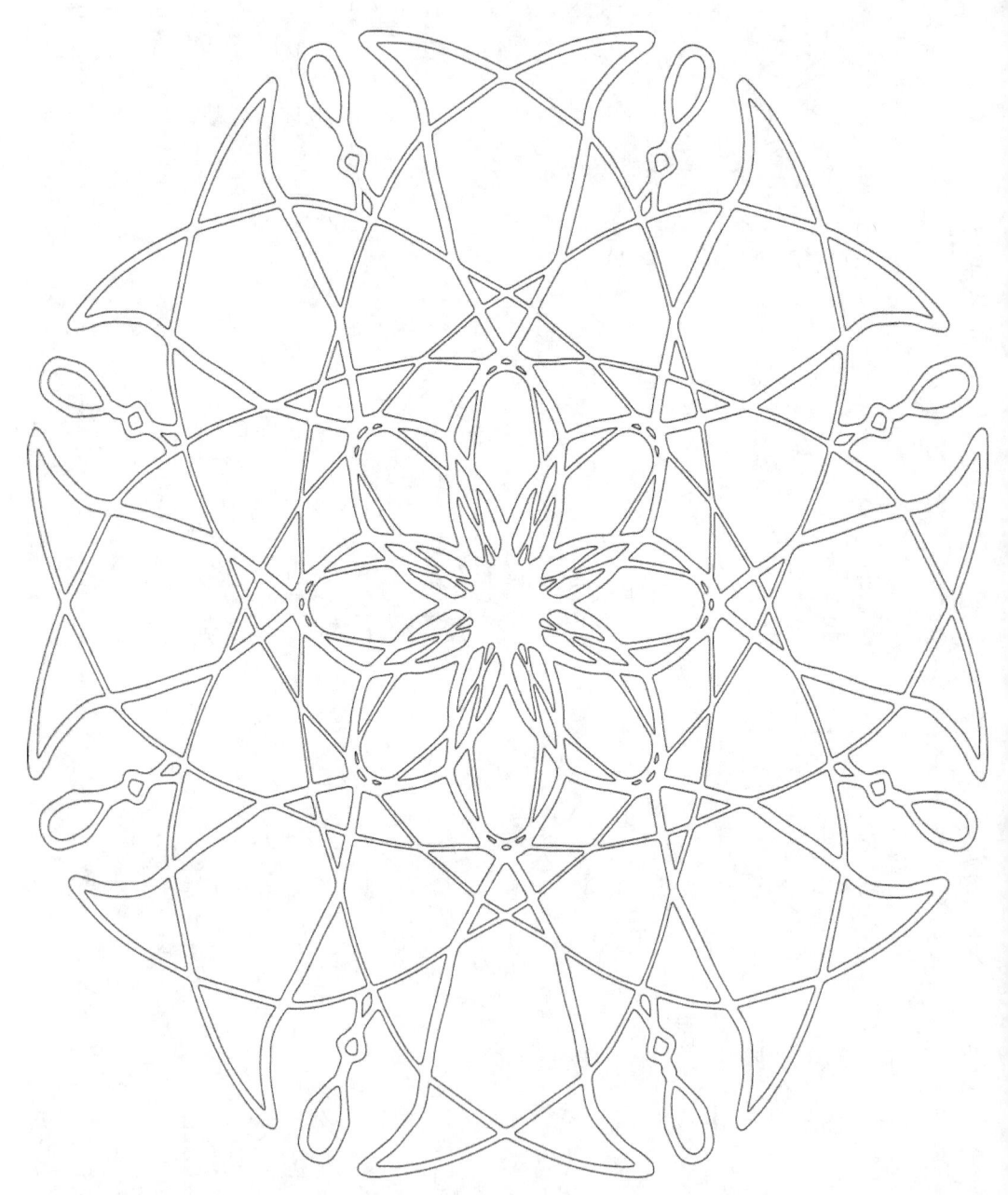

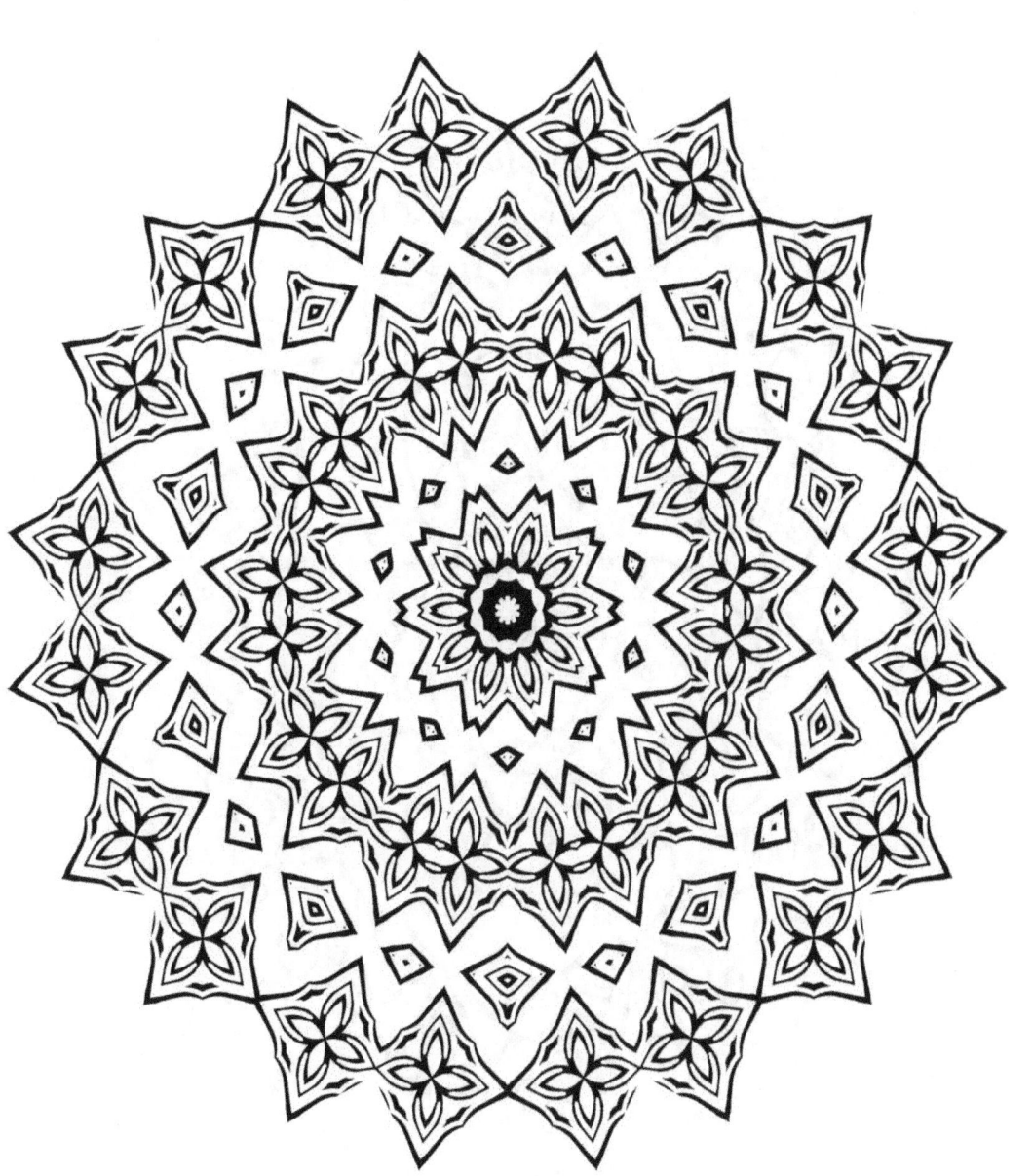

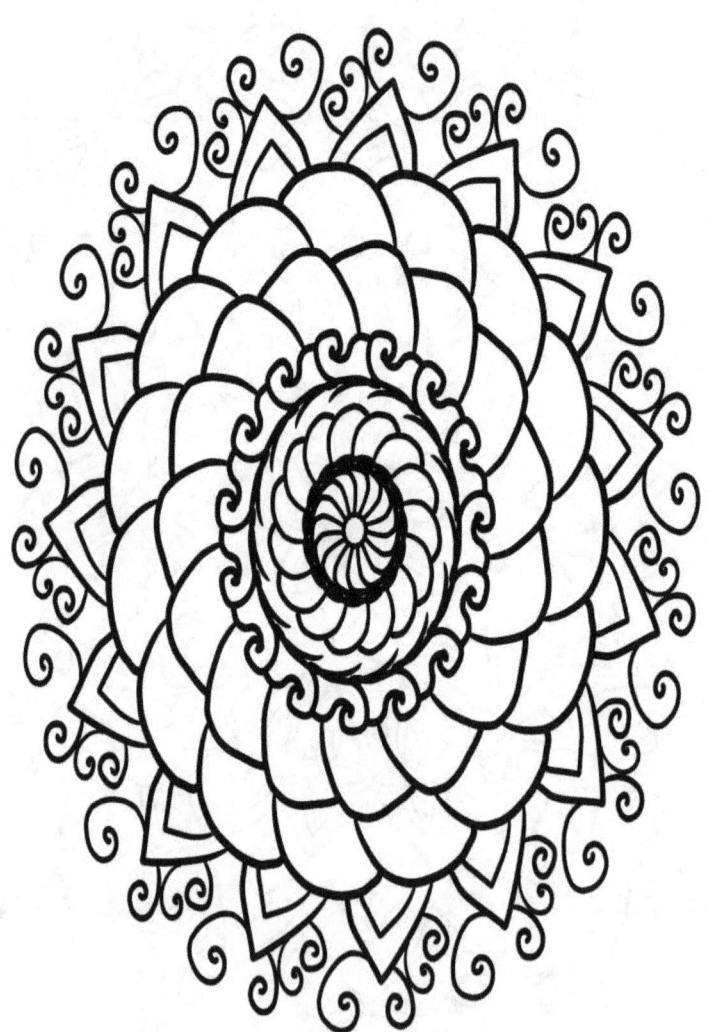

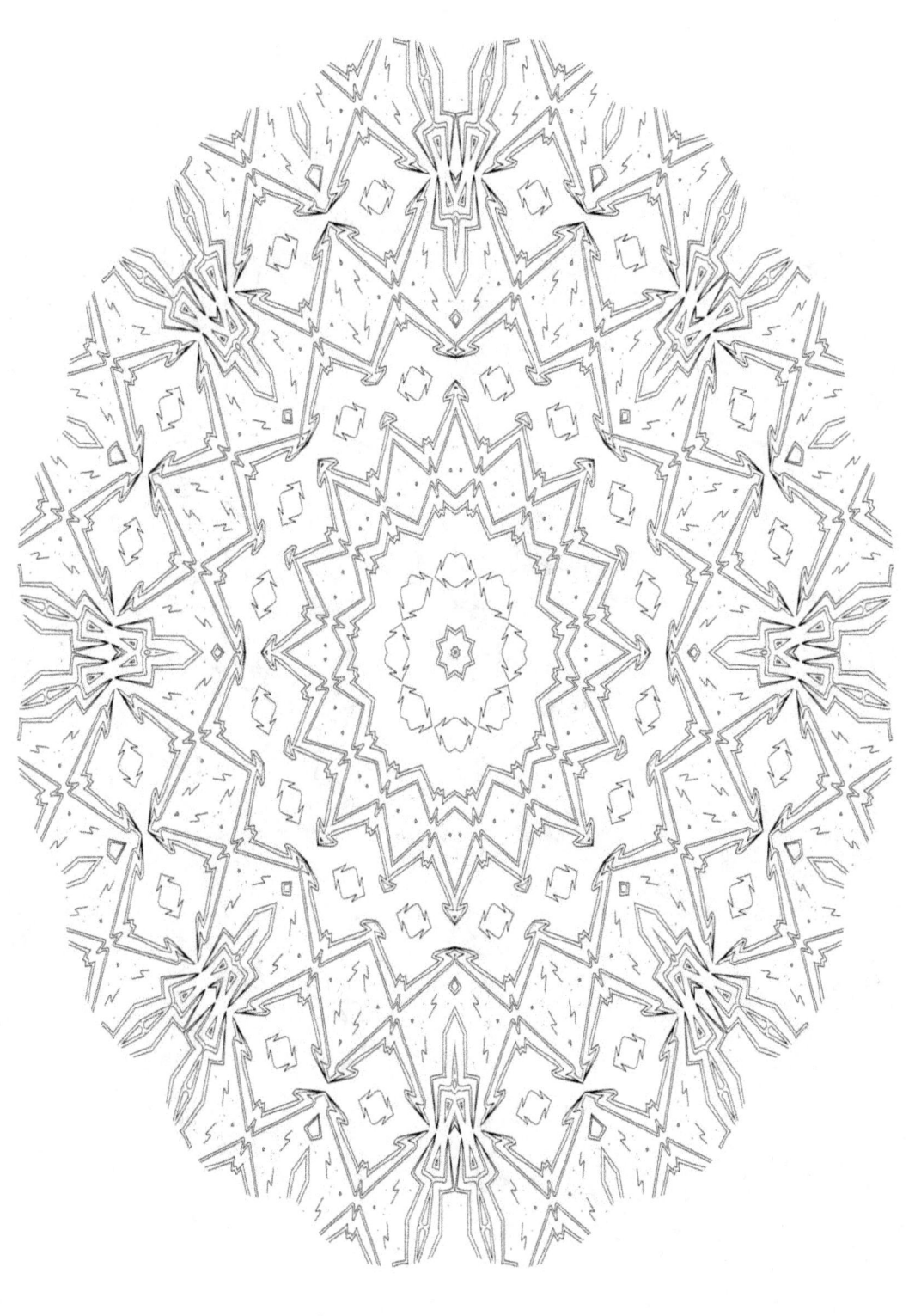

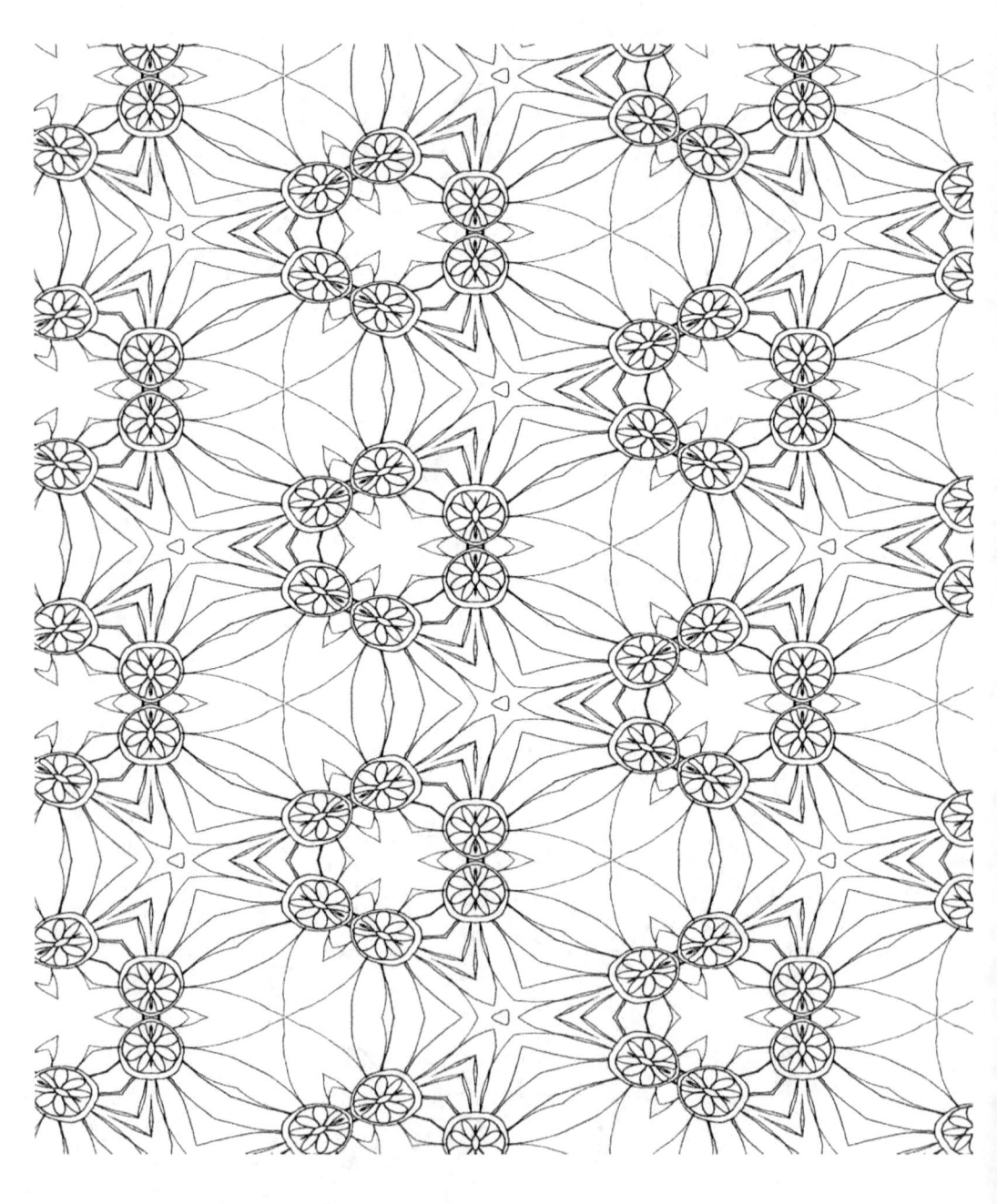

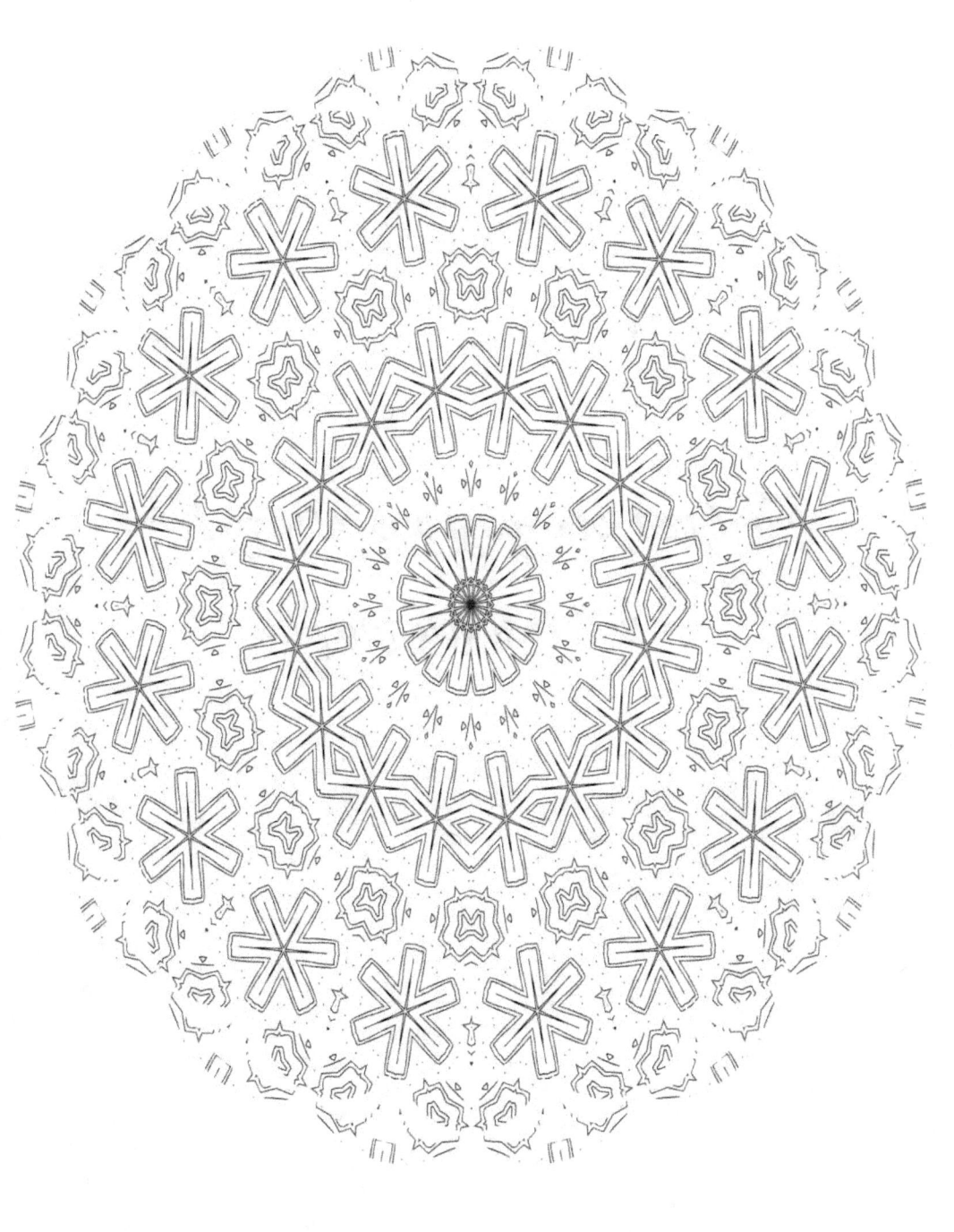

Thank you for buying our coloring book we wish that you had fun.

www.ingramcontent.com/pod-product-compliance
Lightning Source LLC
Chambersburg PA
CBHW050325220526
45465CB00005B/2142